Ugly Pugsy

Written by Julie Connal
Illustrated by Brent Putze

Contents   Page

Nelson

an International Thomson Publishing company ITP®

Ugly Pugsy

With these characters ...

Pugsy

Ann-Marie

Mrs Low

Pete

Angela

"He looks like the sausag

Ugly, pugly Pugsy! Everyone thinks he is the strangest, ugliest dog around. Everyone, that is, except Pugsy's owner, Ann-Marie. She knows how beautiful Pugsy really is, no matter what other people say.

What will it take for poor Pugsy to be the happy and proud dog he should be? How will he realise that to feel good about himself on the *outside*, he needs to feel good on the *inside* first?

had for dinner last night!"

Chapter 1.

Pugsy had a long back, strong short legs, long droopy ears, a proud turned-up nose, and a big bushy tail like a feather duster. Any dog would have been proud to have *one* of these features, but all of them, on the same dog, was most unusual. To most people, Pugsy was an odd, strange-looking animal.

People said Pugsy's long back was too long for his legs. They said Pugsy's strong, short legs were *too* short for his body. People said Pugsy's proud turned-up nose looked like a banana and that his tail was just too long for his body. Some people just thought his ears were too droopy.

Instead of saying, "What a handsome dog," Pugsy heard them saying something quite different.

"Oh, look at that strange-looking dog," they whispered and giggled. "Isn't he ugly?"

But that wasn't the worst part.

When people found out Pugsy's name, they laughed. They said that his name was as ugly as he looked. They said he looked like a 'pugsy' and that he suited his name.

"Ugly, pugly, Pugsy!" the neighbourhood children called out whenever they saw him.

Now, this wouldn't upset too many dogs, but Pugsy was different. He was tired of people teasing him about his odd-looking features. He felt hurt when people talked about him that way. He *felt* ugly!

Those unkind comments made Pugsy's tail
hang, his ears droop even further and his eyes
look sad. Those comments made Pugsy drag his
short legs. People's teasing comments and
laughter made Pugsy look even worse, and his
bushy tail would flop listlessly behind him.

One person never laughed at Pugsy, or called him names. Ann-Marie, Pugsy's owner, loved everything about him.

She loved the way he ran fast on his strong legs.

She loved the way he wriggled his long back in the wet grass.

She loved the way he poked his long nose behind the couch cushions to find toys.

Most of all, she just loved Pugsy—the full package—for who he was.

But it didn't seem to matter how many times Ann-Marie told Pugsy she loved him. It didn't matter how many sticks she threw for Pugsy to chase, or how many times she walked him along the beach so he could play in the waves. Pugsy believed he was ugly. Why else would everyone laugh and point at him?

Pugsy didn't feel good about himself on the inside. If he didn't feel good on the inside, he wasn't going to look good on the outside. But Pugsy *did* feel confident about what to do next!

Chapter 2.

Pugsy started to misbehave. If people weren't going to be nice to him, he wasn't going to be nice to them, either. People's unkind comments made Pugsy want to do naughty things. Pugsy would often run away from home, bark loudly at the person delivering the neighbourhood's mail and, some days, he would saunter around to annoy Mr Bono, the owner of the local Italian bakery.

One morning, when Pugsy was feeling really terrible, he decided to run around to Mr Bono's bakery and bark louder than usual at him. Mr Bono had often pointed at Pugsy in the street and laughed at him. But Pugsy had discovered that barking loudly was a great way to annoy Mr Bono. He enjoyed watching Mr Bono become annoyed and red in the face!

So, that day, Pugsy quietly slipped through his front gate and headed down the road towards the bakery.

It was rubbish day. The normally quiet street was filled with rubbish bins, items for recycling and a huge, noisy rubbish truck. Pugsy's tail drooped, as he slunk past the truck towards Mr Bono's bakery.

"Hey, Pete!" shouted the truck driver, as Pugsy tried to slip by. "There's that weird-looking dog I was telling you about yesterday," he laughed.

"You're right," Pete called back. "He looks like the sausage I had for dinner last night!"

Pugsy felt hurt. "I really am ugly," he thought. His tail drooped even further and his eyes looked sad. Then he became angry.

To annoy the rude rubbish men, he ran straight towards a tall pile of newspapers that Pete had just finished stacking. Before Pete could tip them into the truck, Pugsy scattered them everywhere!

Pete was furious. The rubbish truck driver
shook his fist.

"Go on, get out of here, you ugly mutt!" yelled
Pete to Pugsy.

Pugsy ran as fast as he could, his ears flapping
and his tail drooping. But not before giving a rude
bark back at the rubbish men and their truck.

On his way to the bakery, Pugsy spotted Mrs Low's cat, Cutesy, sitting on a stone wall. He made a low growl, as he turned the corner out of his street and onto the main road. On his way home, he would deal with Cutesy. *Then* she'd get a fright—he would make sure of that! But, right now, he was getting close to Mr Bono's bakery.

As Pugsy started to turn the corner into Wright Street, his head was hanging so low he wasn't watching where he was going.

Pugsy ran straight into a shopping trolley piled high with cat food. He looked back with a whimper and saw that Cutesy's owner, mean old Mrs Low, was waving angrily at him.

She screamed at Pugsy and took a swipe at him.

"You are a clumsy, stupid dog!" she cried. "Someone should clip those silly-looking ears back with a peg so you can see where you're going!"

"Another person who thinks I look ugly,"
growled Pugsy. "I might be ugly, but I *am* clever,"
he thought, deciding not to snarl at Mrs Low.
She would probably snarl back louder and longer!
He bowed his head even lower and stole a
backward glance in Cutesy's direction. The cat
was grinning her cutest cat grin and stepping
daintily along the stone wall, towards Mrs Low.

"Grrrrrrrrrrrrrr," thought Pugsy. "I wish I had
stayed in my kennel this morning."

But it was too late. Pugsy was on a roll of
mishaps, misunderstandings and mistakes.

Pugsy continued, half-running and half-walking,
down the street. Without looking left or right, he
darted across the road, with his head hung low.

Screech! Car brakes were slammed on and a
horn tooted loudly. The driver of the car leant
over and yelled out the window.

"What are you trying to do, you ugly dog?
Want to get your turned-up nose turned down
permanently? You stupid animal! Watch
where you're going!"

Pugsy didn't care what the woman said to him. He had heard so many horrible things about how he looked and behaved that he decided they must be true. He was feeling awful inside. He was hot and thirsty, and he felt like *really* annoying somebody, *anybody*.

With that, Pugsy turned down the lane heading toward Mr Bono's Italian bakery. He slunk past the messy shop backyards until he reached the back entrance of the bakery.

Chapter 3.

When Pugsy sniffed around the back door of the bakery, he could smell bread and cakes cooking. Good! He knew that meant Mr Bono was inside.

Pugsy used all his energy to bark as long and as loudly as he could, hoping that Mr Bono would come out and shoo him away. He half-hoped that Mr Bono would give him a cake, and maybe a bowl of water. But that never happened. Mr Bono was always mean and horrible to Pugsy. As he barked louder and longer, his bark became deeper and croakier.

Suddenly, something unexpected happened. Mr Bono didn't come out.

Instead, his daughter, Angela, appeared at the door, smiling and holding out a hand to Pugsy.

"Well, who are you?" she said to Pugsy in a friendly voice. "Are you singing for me?"

"What a lively character you are," she said, moving closer. "With your fine long back, your strong short legs, your handsome turned-up nose and your big, fluffy tail."

Pugsy listened, stunned into silence. He was so surprised, he forgot to bark. He turned his head to one side to listen to her kind, soothing voice.

"Because I don't know what your name is, I'm going to give you a beautiful Italian name. I'm going to call you Puccini, after a famous Italian composer."

Pugsy didn't know what to do. He had never heard a stranger say nice things about him before. Maybe she was trying to trick him?

"Stay there," said Angela, as she turned to go inside. She came out with something in her hand.

"I am going to tie this gorgeous red scarf around your neck, because it will suit your fine character," she said softly.

Pugsy couldn't believe his ears. He lifted his head and looked at the girl. Maybe she really cared about him? Pugsy felt good.

Angela held out her hand, shook Puccini's paw, and then tied the red scarf gently around his neck. Somewhere, around the back, Pugsy felt a strange movement. He turned around and saw that his tail was wagging.

"That has never happened before," he thought. "I wonder if it will stop?"

"There you are, Puccini," said the girl, shaking his paw. "It was nice to meet you. You are a beautiful dog, with a beautiful name."

Puccini was overjoyed. This girl, a complete stranger, had called him a *beautiful* dog! She had given him a beautiful name, and a beautiful, bright red scarf. He felt handsome in his new red scarf, with his beautiful Italian name. He turned to trot proudly and happily towards home, with his head and tail held high.

Chapter 4.

"Of course," thought Puccini to himself, "people won't recognise me, looking so handsome in this scarf. It is so beautiful. I feel so proud."

He trotted up the lane, his shoulders back and his head held high. His nose, slightly raised, sniffed the air proudly, and he wore his red scarf at a jaunty angle.

With his red scarf tied around his neck, Puccini felt like a famous dog!

He reached the end of the lane.

Instead of darting across the busy main road, head down, holding his breath and just hoping for the best, Puccini paused. He sat at the pedestrian crossing and watched all the admiring looks of people in the passing cars.

A car stopped, and Puccini grandly and proudly crossed the road.

A girl in the back seat smiled and waved at Puccini.

"Hey, Mum, look at that *cool* dog!"

Puccini couldn't believe his ears. He felt good inside and, somehow, he just *knew* he looked good on the outside.

He gaily pranced on down the road.

He trotted past Pete, the garbage collector, and the rubbish truck driver. Pete courteously stood back and let Puccini pass.

"Good morning, Mister Dog," he chimed. "You're a perky one."

"Yes, I sure am," thought Puccini. "What a difference a little red scarf can make!"

Puccini rounded the corner into his quiet street. He saw Mrs Low standing there, gossiping to her neighbour, with Cutesy looking very self-satisfied in her arms.

But nothing could ruin Puccini's moment. He trotted by, secure in the knowledge his scarf was making him look just fine, thank you very much.

"Well, well, well. What a transformation!" said Mrs Low. "What's happened to you, Pugsy?"

"It's *Puccini*, thank you," thought Puccini to himself.

And for just one moment, which Puccini really enjoyed, Cutesy no longer looked like a cat that thought she was the best-looking animal around.

In fact, she looked exactly the opposite. Puccini felt so gracious that he didn't even growl, as he had planned to do earlier.

Puccini happily trotted through his front gate, and even collected the paper between his teeth on his way to the front door.

If he could have, he would have whistled. Instead, he held his head high and wagged his big, fluffy tail all the way up to the door.

Chapter 5.

When Ann-Marie heard Pugsy barking at the front door, she opened it and cried out.

"Thank goodness you're back, Pugsy. I've been looking for you everywhere!" she exclaimed.

Pugsy was amazed. "How does she know it's me?" he wondered.

"I thought you had been causing trouble again, but it looks as though something else has happened. You look ... different, somehow," said Ann-Marie, staring at her dog.

"I sure do," thought Puccini.

"You look so happy and perky," said Ann-Marie curiously. "You look so confident. You look positively gorgeous."

Puccini stood still, as he showed off his best angle. He wanted this moment to last forever. He waited patiently for Ann-Marie to compliment him on his beautiful red scarf.

But Ann-Marie said nothing.

Puccini waited.

But still Ann-Marie said nothing.

So, finally, Pugsy wagged his tail and dipped his head to show her the scarf.

In a moment of panic, he realised that the scarf was no longer there. His beautiful red scarf was gone! He was devastated.

His face drooped, his ears drooped, his head drooped, his nose lost that proud tilt and his tail stopped wagging.

"Why, Pugsy, what's wrong?" asked Ann-Marie.

It was then that Puccini realised that he hadn't been wearing the scarf when all those people had admired and complimented him.

He hadn't had the scarf on when the girl had said he was a cool dog. He hadn't had the scarf on when the rubbish men had treated him so nicely. He hadn't had the scarf on when Mrs Low had spoken to him. He hadn't looked different. He had only been acting differently.

He smiled, lifted his head, puffed his chest out, put his shoulders back and lifted his nose to a jaunty angle. He waved his fluffy tail proudly.

"You know that you're my favourite dog, no matter what people say about you," said Ann-Marie affectionately. "You are unique!"

Pugsy smiled. He wasn't 'ugly, pugly Pugsy' anymore. He was a happy, proud dog and he felt good, inside and out. He was 'unique', and he didn't even need a beautiful red scarf or a beautiful name to prove it. He just needed to be himself and to be happy with who he was.

Pugsy was home.

"A beautiful red scarf."

Pugsy
Ugly, sad
Flopping, barking, slinking
Legs, tail, ears, scarf
Trotting, wagging, grinning
Proud, happy
Puccini!